oh,
boy

to fix a broken T.V.
is something I never could do
to fix a broken arm
↓
to fix a broken !
↓
to transplant a broken liver,   SURGEON
that, could not do.
to fix a broken radio,   ELECTRICIAN
~~I'd~~ I don't not know where to ~~begin~~. START

to ~~fix~~ GOVERN

~~to play on a~~ ↯↯↯↯↯↯↯↯↯

~~↯↯↯~~

to fly a passenger plane   PILOT
I'd be scared just half to death.
to work for politics
oh I'd be so very bored

That's
way   I'm so GLAD ~~not~~ that everyone
is not ~~alike~~ the same as me

'cause surgeons, electricians, pilots and governors
oh ~~they~~ there just ~~would~~ would not ever ~~rise~~

→

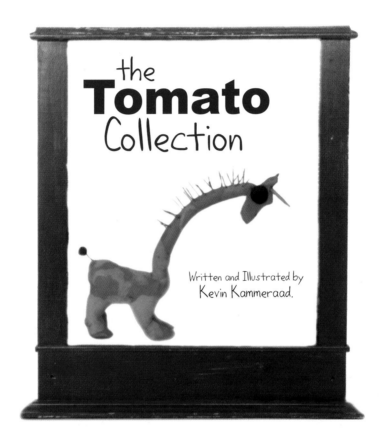

the
Tomato
Collection

Written and Illustrated by
Kevin Kammeraad.

to Sheldon Woods!

Kevin Kammeraad

Magpooie :
Achoogie + zileeto

tree [1]   [2]   flowers   [3]   [4]   wizard hat   [5]   [6]   tree

- one long Landscape Bookmarked by trees
- ~~Oil~~ Painting
ACRYLIC
- done to size 8'½ x 11
- Put a little critter on Page 6?

Cooperfly Books
THE TOMATO COLLECTION Copyright © 1999 by Kevin Kammeraad.
Summary: 64 pages of poetry and artwork with many topics and media.

Many whimsical glimpses into a young child's psyche are captured in this delightful collection. Questions, observations, fantasies, frivolities, and just plain "funny thoughts" are presented in word and living color. Hopefully, the readers will not only enjoy the verse and the art, but be challenged to create their own poetry and pictures.
   - *K Laurel Balkema,* Children's and Young Adult Literature Collection Librarian - Grand Valley State University

Publisher's Cataloging-in-Publication Data
Kammeraad, Kevin.
     The tomato collection / written and illustrated
   by Kevin Kammeraad -- 1st ed.
     p. cm.
     Includes index.
     LCCN 98-
     ISBN 0-9669504-0-2

     1. Children's poetry, American   I. Title.

   PZ8.3.K12575To 1999   [E]
     Z277 4/99   QBI98-1750

Technical and Creative Assistance: Kyle Hofmeyer, Idiom Productions, Inc.
Book Production Coordinator: Thomas M. Vranich, Bookability, Inc.
Photography: Steve Kammeraad, Kammeraad Photography (and we think he took most of the family photo snapshots).
Our thanks to Margaret Proctor for her editorial assistance as well as to the many people who have offered their support.

Printed in Hong Kong
10 9 8 7 6 5 4 3 2 1

For my parents, Steve and Linda and for my sisters, Kristi and Lori.

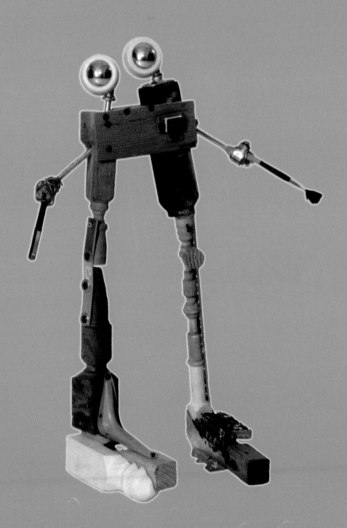

4

Frogs and Toads.

a crocodile is not a 'gator
a wasp is not a bee
a frog is not a toad
a bush is not a tree.
i just don't see the difference
it's hard for me to see
but i really know for sure
a you is not a me.

Jacob's Poem.

can you *see* 'em?
do you *see* 'em?
they gotta be around.
can you *see* 'em?
do you *see* 'em?
up and down,
and all around,
they *simply* must be found!
to the left,
to the right,
up and down,
day and night.
can you *see* 'em?
do you *see* 'em?
they gotta be around.
can you *see* 'em?
do you *see* 'em?
they *simply* must be found!

Stronger Pushers.

our car has lost a tire
it doesn't move too fast
we tried to push real hard
but we only came in last;
for we tried to win a race
with a car without a tire!
but now we know what to do
stronger pushers we will hire.

Natalie.

natalie sat in her bed and began to think. she thought of the little squirrel who bought a big red car to drive to the ocean. she thought of fourteen laughing turtles building sand castles. she dreamed of clowns who wear business suits and sing about coffee tables as they make those "balloon animal things."

natalie sat in her bed and dreamed.

Noonies.

i sit and eat my noonies
they're filling up my tummy,
i eat them every day
they taste so very yummy.
now some of you may wonder
what actually is a noonie?
and some of you may think
that i'm a little loony.
but a noonie is a noodle
covered up with cheese,
so i'd like to go on eating
my noonies if you please.

Joe.

"hey joe,
can you hand me that tape?"
"sorry,
i just ate the last grape."
"hey joe,
can i borrow a dollar?"
"yes,
i guess, but what do you do with a collar?"
"hey joe,
you wanna go to the game?"
"sure,
i'd love to ride a train."
"hey joe!
are you feeling okay?"
"sounds great,
see ya friday!"

A Tree Without a Trunk.

a lake without the water
tomorrow without today
a song without a sound
and june without first may.
oh, it'd be a crazy thing
if everything was this way
but "maybe it will happen"
im sure that some will say.

11

The Sun Will Always Float.

when i worry about getting teased
and people being mean to me,
i remember,
the sun will always float.

when i'm afraid of being alone
and no one else is there,
i remember,
the sun will always float.

when i'm sad because i've lost a friend
who had to die too soon,
i remember,
the sun will always float.

and when i'm just plain scared,
i remember,
the sun will always float.

Concert of
the Blind.

the cruel rhythm of the voices
they tear apart the heart,
the soul, the mind.
this yelling, screaming and fighting
create the concert of the blind,
for so many do not see
the power of what's heard.
for it does not take a weapon
or the fist,
but simply,
only the spoken word.

13

Well Hey.

i'm feeling kinda down,
i don't know why
but i know it's true.
but why or what
should i do?
some say cry,
a few say bye
or maybe lie,
but i think that i'll
go on and try.

14

29 Cookies.

ate far too much
my stomach's far too full!
i'm feeling kinda funny
not feeling very well.
i knew i should have stopped
but they all just taste so great
it's the 28th cookie,
i just should not have ate.

How to Cook an Egg.

1. raise a chicken and name her meg.

2. wait for your chicken to lay an egg.

3. find a pan and find a stove.

4. turn the heat on very low.

5. now put that egg right in your pan.

6. wait around, just sit or stand.

7. once she's hatched, you'll be happy to see,

8. there's a chirping addition to your family.

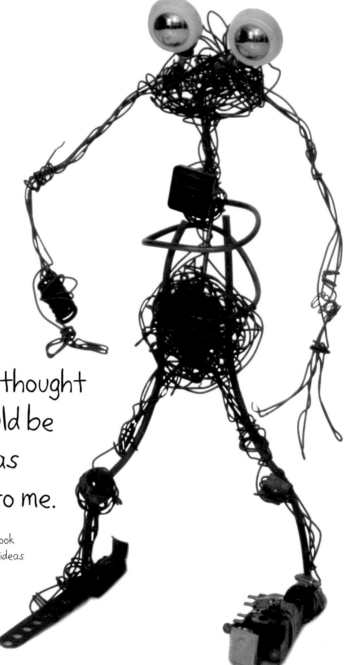

Norwood.

i thought and thought and thought
of what this poem should be
i wrote down my ideas
but none seemed right to me.

(Norwood's a little bit embarrassed that he's in the book
without a "real" poem. He would like it if anyone has any ideas
to please write him a "real" poem.)

Opening Gifts.

i'm opening up my gifts,
and i really hope i like them
'cause i don't like pretending.

'cause no matter what it is
i'll surely say "it's nice,"
but i'll know you only bought it
'cause it had a cheapy little price.

but i'll sit and hold my smile
just waiting for it to end,
and when again you ask
"you really like it?"
i'll go and say yes again.

id finish this poem
but first id have to start
so rather instead
i think ill call it art.

20

Broken Sled.

rapidly sledding down
and running back up top,
we are always going
we will never stop!
flying like a jet
over the jumps we hop.
the speed only...OOPS!
i think i heard a pop
oh well,
i guess it's time to stop.

oh, boy

turn to the left, quick!

look out!

hold on!

Sleeper People.

the sleeper people,
they help me to go to sleep.
i sit in bed each night
and listen for them.
but tonight,
i don't hear their whispers.
yet somehow,
very, very slowly
(you see they're in no hurry)
they will make my eyes heavy
and then i'll sleep
as they wake up.

22

Cookie Batch.

i ate some shortening
i ate 2 eggs
i ate the butter
and ate brown sugar
i ate some salt
and ate some vanilla
chocolate chips
and 2 cups of flour.
now i'm sure you're thinking
this doesn't sound too great
but when you put it all together
a batch of cookies i just ate.

....natalie dreamed of moving to a place happier than butterflies with chocolate milk. she dreamed of running faster than a cheetah with a cheeseburger. she dreamed of making a movie about green ants who don't like the winter so they fly to hawaii from november to may.

natalie sat in her bed and dreamed.

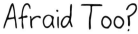

Afraid Too?

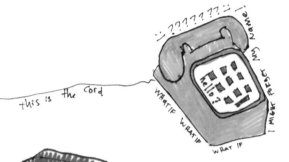

this is the cord

AFRAID

im afraid to make that call
what if she laughs at me?
i'd have to hide my face
in a place that she might be.

im afraid to make that call
what if she thinks im dumb?
then every time i see her
i'd have to turn and run.

im afraid to make that call
and may always be alone.
but the thing that makes it sad:
she may be waiting by the phone.

Maybe if i write down what to say

Me hiding

HA HA

Me hiding

Phone Call

RUN
RUN RUN

Where are you?

Me

Little Low One.

whenever i go to the bathroom
and see two urinals;
one up high
and one down low,
i always take the high one.
i remember once
my teacher came in,
he had to use the little low one.
i had to laugh,
because even though he is smarter
and bigger,
i had the good one.

my
teacher

The Couch.

the couch has eaten my friend!
i don't know what to do
beware, it could happen to you.

hey, that couch ate my friend!
im afraid to say it's true
but it ate my sister too.

that mean old couch!
i hope you know what to do
if it ever happens to you.

well that's my story
about the couch that ate my friend.
but don't worry
it's really just pretend.

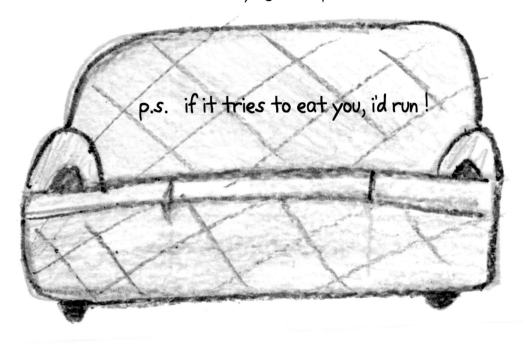

p.s. if it tries to eat you, i'd run !

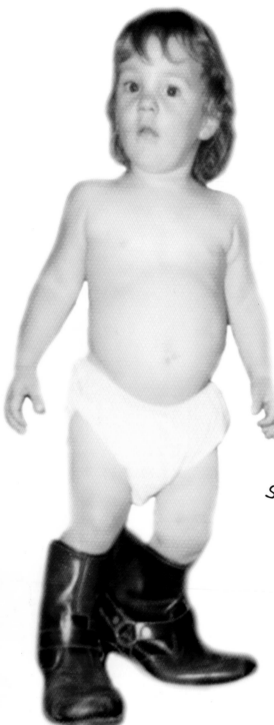

Pumpkin Belly.

soon,
there will be pumpkins in my belly,
as soon as the seeds grow.
i know it's gonna happen
i really really know.
for i've been eating pumpkin seeds
'cause they taste just really great
so when there's a pumpkin
in my belly,
it's 'cause the seeds
i just now ate.

Quitter.

i could paint a beautiful painting,
of happy thoughts and smiling bananas.
but it could look funny,
so i'll quit now.

i could write an incredible book,
about giraffes and mice.
but it might not turn out,
so i'll quit now.

i could have a terrific job,
where i'd sell cookies to the world for a penny.
but i could get fired,
so i'll quit now.

i could find a cure for all bad sicknesses
and find a way to save miss micknesses.
but that's too much work,
so i'll quit now.

what's that you say?
it's crazy to think this way?
but it's so much easier
and safer to think this way.
you still don't agree!
you think i need to follow my heart?
you're absolutely right
it's time for me to start.

Chilly Billy.

mark says he's brilly
shannon says she's zilly
beth thinks she's dilly
and billy says he's chilly
but come on billy!
that's just silly.

Here and There.

over here
and then over there
and when i'm there
i forget about here.
and when doing this
i forget about that
and all about this
and this and that.

Ice Cubes.

i've come today
i'm here to complain
about one thing,
it's a real big pain.
it's that last ice cube
that won't slide out.
you just can't give up
as it stays in place,
then sure enough
it's in your face.

Better?

better to see than to hear
better to be than to mirror
better to forget than to fear
and better to glide than to steer?

First Things First.

i could have been a doctor
and saved a life.
i could have been a lawyer
and protected a life.
i could have been a movie star
and portrayed a life.
or i could have been a me
and lived a life.

Stuck With a Frown.

option one
option two
neither good
what to do?
option one
option two
daily dilemma
nothing new.

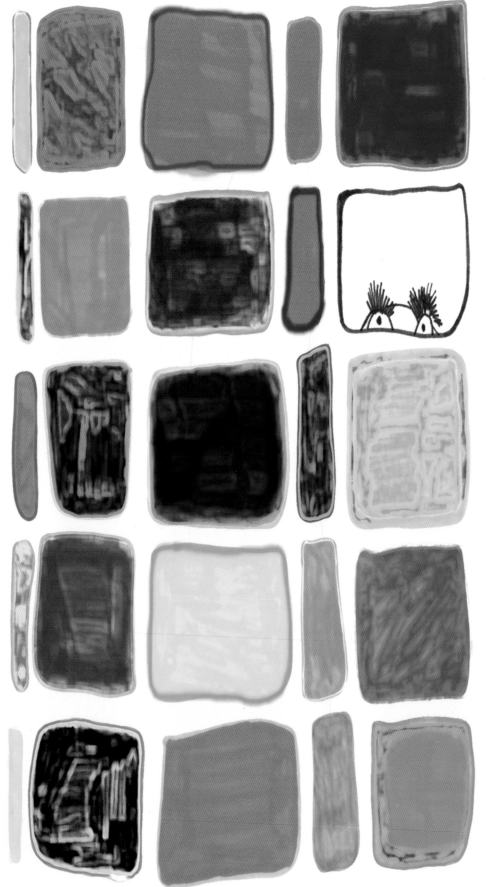

Eyebrow Trick.

they say that
going bald
comes from
your mother's dad.
so if that is
really true
well, i don't
have a chance.
so i've decided
not to wait,
the time to
act is now.
so what i'm
going to do,
is grow out
each eyebrow.
and once they've
grown out long,
i'll comb 'em back
real slick,
and then i'll
look real good!
feel free to use
my trick.

Alphabet Rain.

it's raining capital Z's
and lower case b's
a couple of D's
and a few little c's
it's a crazy thing
i'm getting all wet
not cats and dogs
but the alphabet!

33

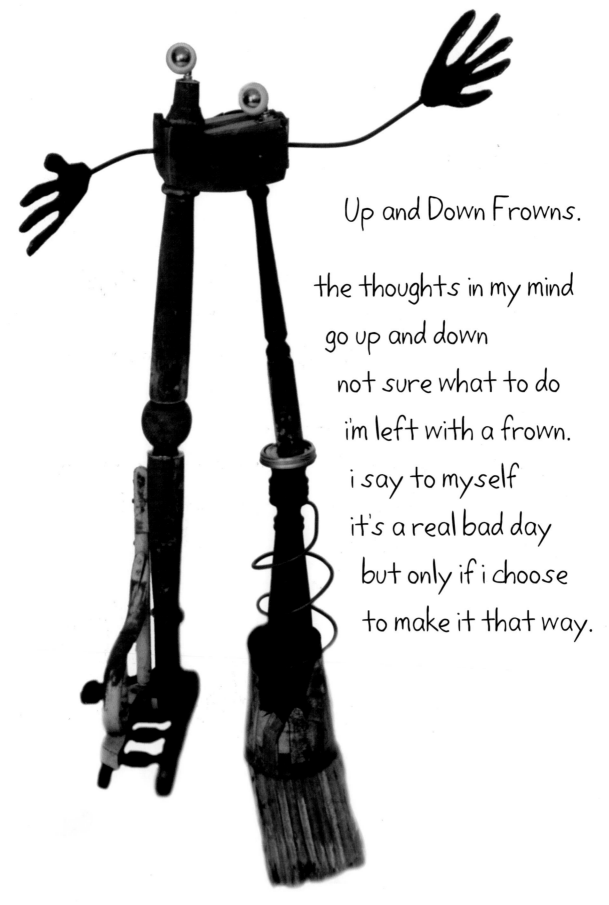

Up and Down Frowns.

the thoughts in my mind
go up and down
not sure what to do
i'm left with a frown.
i say to myself
it's a real bad day
but only if i choose
to make it that way.

Positively, Absolutely.

why?
why am i the only person to feel this way?
no one else has ever felt like this.
i am positively the only person to ever have to
go through this.
nobody else has ever been afraid,
afraid of the growling chipmunks under the bed.
i am definitely the only one in the world
to feel this feeling.
positively, absolutely.

Dinner.

for fish
ate carrots
to squash
one pie.

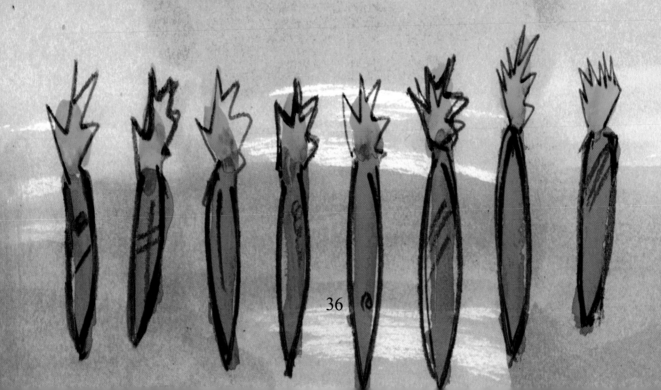

The Best Poem Ever.

i had an incredible idea!
it would have been the world's best poem ever!
    (but i forgot it)
i guess i'll just think of a better one,
    maybe about elephants,
elephants that eat little cheese crackers.

...natalie dreamed of angels with bashful flowers and silent wings dancing around her. she dreamed of living in massachusetts and owning her own brownie farm. she thought of taking a vacation and walking to outer space to visit her sister.

natalie sat in her bed and dreamed.

Sun and Moon.

i really don't know for sure
but i really hope it's true
that the sun and moon are dating
oh don't you hope so too?
but they live so far away
and i guess they're all alone
but i know that it could work
if they only had a phone.
but they'd make a perfect pair!
im sure you do agree
so i know there is a reason
why it isn't meant to be.

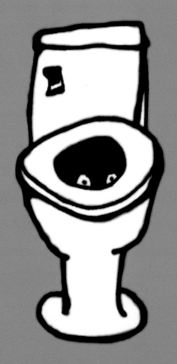

Little Man Jay.

you may not believe me
but my uncle says it's true
there's a man inside the toilet
his job's no fun to do!
for he has to sit and wait
for people to take a seat
his job is to hold the pail
and keep the toilet neat.

Moogie Monster Man.

the moogie monster man
broke into my room
and the moogie monster man
made a mess, stole my broom.
so i don't think it's fair
it's another parent scam
'cause i didn't make the mess
it was the moogie monster man.

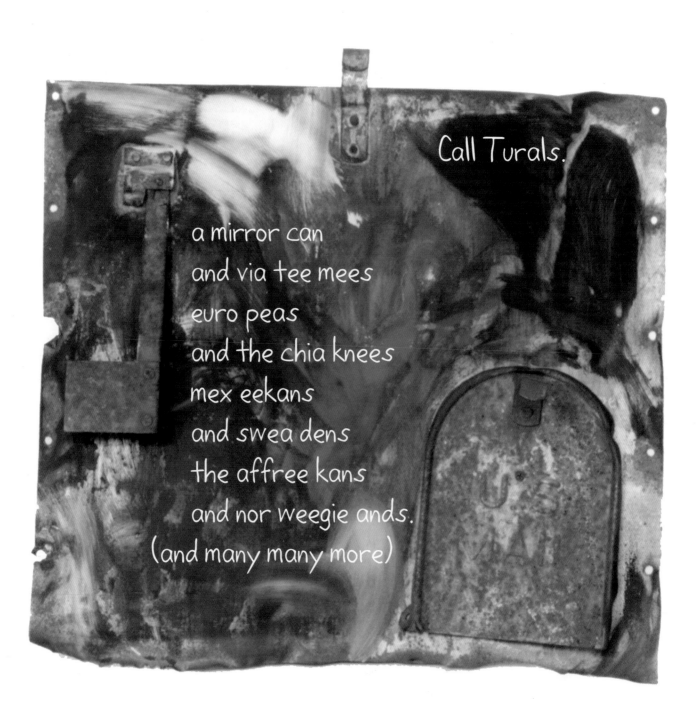

Call Turals.

a mirror can
and via tee mees
euro peas
and the chia knees
mex eekans
and swea dens
the affree kans
and nor weegie ands.
(and many many more)

Impressions
of Each Other.

i have an impression of you
and you have an impression of me
but the impression you have of me
that i'll never see.
another way to put that
is i know what i think of you
but what someone thinks of me
in that position, i will never be.

43

To My Family and Friends.

life's a funny thing
for there is no guarantee
that we'll live to see tomorrow
it can end just instantly.
but there are so many things
that i would like to say
before it is decided
that today is now my day.
mostly, i want to say "i love you"
to my family and my friends.
we've shared the best of times
too bad it has to end.
and yes,
i know it is no fun
to think about this stuff
but those little words "i love you"
i just don't say enough.

Grouchy.

i hang upside down
to lose my grouchy frown.

Remote Control.
   the remote is there
      but i am here
   so i'm sure you see
   and share my fear,
   for i'd have to get up
      to watch t.v.
   so i'm stuck in silence
      oh man, why me!

...natalie dreamed of ice cream shaped bears that play the trumpet. she thought of climbing a mountain of tapioca pudding. she dreamed that everyone with cancer was cured throughout the world. she dreamed of frogs that fall in love with dragon flies.

natalie sat in her bed and dreamed.

Sweet
Pea Emily.

there's a girl,
a girl next to me.
she's sitting two chairs down.
she's cute
as cute as can be
and sweet
as sweet as a pea
as sweet as a pea can be.

Thanks.

sometimes life is tough
and mean
and sad
and angry
and loud,
but god is taking care of me.

Magooie and Achoogie.

Here's a little story
about Magooie Balooie,
a baboon raccoon
and Achoogie Aboogie,
a chunky monkey.
They swimmed and they swam,
they runned and they ran,
they hipped and they hopped,
and they bipped and they bopped.

But then one day
Papa Wizard, the magical lizard, declared:
"You are to have no more fun!"
"What!" said Magooie.
"What do we do?" cried Achoogie.

So the days went on and everything was quiet.
  Nobody runned.
Nobody ran.
  Nobody swimmed.
Nobody swam.

Then Magooie said to Achoogie
"Something must be done."
"Yes, something must be done!" said Achoogie.
So they went to solve the problem of
Papa Wizard, the magical lizard.
After four and a half days of scheming and
planning and planning and scheming
they finally had a plan.

At 4:10pm on a Thursday,
Magooie and Achoogie trapped
Papa Wizard, the magical lizard,
in the center of town.

With the help of Zaleeto Braleeto,
Talooka Shalooka, Neeno Daleeno and
Superfly Cooperfly, they all played, laughed,
cheered and sang as loud as they could!
The fun was so incredible that Papa Wizard
had no choice but to sing and dance along.

So once again
  Magooie and Achoogie and everyone else,
they swimmed and they swam,
they runned and they ran,
  they hipped and they hopped,
  and they bipped and they bopped.

53

Other Side Inside.

i've often heard
that beauty lies inside.
in my case
i know they haven't lied,
'cause on the outside
it can be a scary sight;
but on my other side
it's really rather bright.

Wholly See.

four, sun,
to and so.
why oh why?
i don't know.
for, son,
two and sew.
any sense?
i say no.
whole, be,
roll and tea.
oh, it's crazy.
only me?
hole, bee,
role and tee.
guess i never
will holy sea.

Sloppy Sloopy Slop.

the winter can be great
there's lots of stuff to do
like sledding, skating, skiing
and building snowmen too.
but we could do without that time
after winter (before the spring)
'cause that sloppy sloopy slop
is such a sloppy thing.

If Everyone was Just Like Me.

to transplant a broken liver
i could not do for you.
to fix a broken car
i couldn't do that too.
to be a politician
i'd never want to do!
if i said i want to be a lawyer
that's no where close to true.
but i'm thankful everyone else
is not the same as me
'cause surgeons, mechanics,
mayors and lawyers
oh, there just would never be.

natalie left her bed to live her dreams.

Index:

The Tomato Family:

The giraffe on the title page is Ned Vander Bosh. He enjoys playing the electric guitar. The little guy on the dedication page is Bradford, who is the cousin of Norwood (on page 17). The guy from "Up and Down Frowns" (on page 34) is Norwood's father, Ethan. Both Bradford and Norwood as well as Ethan all enjoy making movies. Those crazy guys Edson and Hewlett (in the blue car on page 4) were on their way to go mountain biking when they said I could take their picture for the book (I later saw them going back home because they forgot their bikes). The bee flying above them is Dex (he's Edson's nephew). The guy on "Jacob's Poem" (on page 6) is, of course, Jacob. He is somewhat shy. Natalie (on page 8) is really good friends with Afraid Too Lou (on page 25). They both like to paint and work on cars. Joe (on page 10) is a good friend of Zaleeto Braleeto. Every Monday they go bowling. The pigeon (on page 11) is a clothing designer and spends a lot of time in France. The angels from "The Sun will Always Float" (on page 12) are working their hardest to keep everyone safe. The "Concert of the Blind" guys (on page 13) did not want to wear red pants for their picture but I told them it would nicely match the colors from "The Sun Will Always Float." They understood completely (but if you ever see them in town, they'll probably be wearing blue jeans). The guy from "Well Hey" (on page 14) likes to go by the name "The Well Hey Guy." He lives in Yelapa. The chicken from "How to Cook an Egg" (on page 16) is Meg. She spends most of her day studying. She hopes to become the Governor of Michigan. The photo shoot for "Broken Sled" (on page 20) was safely monitored and done by a professional stunt man. Don't worry, the people at the bottom of the hill were in no danger. The little bee saying "Oh boy" is an English teacher who happened to be on the set and volunteered to help out. The giraffe from "Quitter" (on page 29) is John. He's the best friend of the Alpha Ant (on page 33) who is the cousin of the Moogie Monster Man (on page 41). The mouse from "Quitter" is a body builder training for the Olympics. His name is James. The group on "Page 30 Poems" are a hockey team (their record last year was only 2 and 8, but they just love to play) and they all play the drums. The guy on "Eyebrow Trick" (on page 32) is the brother of Mr. Conner who is the teacher from "Little Low One" (on page 26). The "Positively, Absolutely" chipmunks (on page 35) are both excellent at water skiing and also enjoy line dancing. The four fish from "Dinner" (on page 36) are Riley, Monroe, Lakewood and Tyler. They are currently busy as tour guides in Lake Michigan. "The Best Poem Ever" elephant (on page 37) is Newman Manewman, who is a good friend of Talooka Shalooka. Newman once almost stepped on the growling chipmunks but the chipmunks hollered "Hey, there's growling little chipmunks down here!" Newman apologized and gave them some crackers. Natalie has offered to give cordless phones to both the sun and the moon (on page 39) on the next trip she takes to visit her sister. Little Man Jay (on page 40) has moved to Oklahoma and is enjoying a new home in the country. The kids from "Impressions of Each Other" (on page 43) are an upcoming rock band who call themselves "The Impressions." Unfortunately, one of "The Impressions" was almost eaten by the couch (on page 27) last week. He is recovering nicely however. I'm proud to say that Magooie and Achoogie are working on a book of their own at this time, Papa Wizard is currently building a new playground on Fuller Street, Neeno Daleeno has moved south (not far, so everyone visits often) and Superfly Cooperfly will forever live on in memory (we'll miss you but you're in a better place). And that's pretty much the family story.

-OOPS!

Author's Notes:

I had no idea that a simple journal would be the start of what is now the **Tomato** Collection.

In December of 1994, my grandmother gave me a notebook for Christmas. For some reason I began to write down what I guess you could call a journal. I filled that journal with thoughts, feelings and ideas regarding my life and have since filled five notebooks. Those notebooks (as shown on the index page) are the books from which the Tomato Collection was created. Over a period of 4 years (in no particular order) I wrote over 700 pages of drafts, revised those drafts, decided which ones to include in the book, added titles, produced the artwork by drawing and painting new stuff, looked through art I had already created, built new sculptures, looked through old photo albums, gradually "assembled" the book on a computer, asked many people for their opinions and revised some more. Then one evening in December of 1998, I finally said "It's done."

I wanted the artwork not to directly "illustrate" the poetry, but to add another level of interpretation. In many cases, it is intended to be abstract to encourage your own imagination. Instead of showing Natalie's dreams, I wanted you to visualize your own thoughts of what they should be. What does Magooie, the Moogie Monster Man, or someone who just finished eating 28 cookies look like? I also want to encourage you to draw those pictures, build sculptures for them or use any style of art you would like to.

I came up with the title of this book mainly for one reason . When I'm writing and get stuck for an idea, a word or a concept, etc., the first word that pops in my mind is the word tomato. I have no idea why.

 The photos of the children are my sisters, Kristi and Lori, and myself when we were little.

Some thoughts on some of the poetry or artwork:

Noonies: My friend Angie Marion refers to her macaroni and cheese as "noonies." This poem was inspired by her. Norwood: Norwood was built out of one big piece of wire, some bolts, springs and odds and ends that my friend's grandmother had in her garage (for some reason she didn't want them). Also, if you write a poem or story for Norwood, I'd love for you to send me a copy (the address and e-mail address are on the last page). "The Art Poem" (on page 19): One of the greatest things about art is the process and time spent creating it. Sleeper People: The stuffed animal on the left is mine, the one on the right is my grandmother's. The Couch: A past roommate of mine, Bill Wendt, said I should write a poem about a "people-eating couch." Pumpkin Belly: Sorry Lori, the picture was just too funny not to use. Eyebrow Trick: This one was inspired by some advice my grandfather gave me a long time ago. Up and Down Frowns: Ethan was built out of old furniture pieces I bought at a garage sale and some stuff I had around the house. Part of his left foot is the bottom of my old mailbox. Of all the poems in this book, this was the first one I wrote (page 4 of the first journal). Dinner: Read it out loud if you're not sure what it means. The Best Poem Ever: Sometimes you just don't have a pen. Sun and Moon: My friend and business partner Kyle Hofmeyer said I should write a poem as if the sun and moon were dating. Call Turals: I painted the rest of my old mailbox for this poem. Remote Control: You should be reading, running, writing, swimming, drawing or bopping anyway. Sweet Pea Emily: I never did dare talk to her (she sat near me in a Geology class). Magooie and Achoogie: My friend Andy Holtgrieve helped me in revising this one. Wholly See: How on earth do we ever learn English? It was another idea from Kyle. Sloppy Sloopy Slop: My friend Bill Kenner said I should write a poem about the sloppy Michigan weather.

About the Author and Artist:

Kevin Kammeraad is always thinking of ways to create or write something new. He enjoys trying different styles when writing and creating "art." Most of the time they change in the process and turn out much differently than when he first began. Kevin also does work in film/video production and enjoys spinach dip.
For more information, see www.tomatocollection.com

Thank You:
The following people have helped me greatly. Without these people, the **Tomato** Collection would not be what it is today:

Thank you to my mother and father. Thank you for all your support and for your love.

Thank you to Kyle Hofmeyer. The computer worked (most of the time) thanks to you and your support on building, designing, creating, upgrading, improving things and running the companies have made the Tomato Collection much greater than it would have been.

Thank you to all the teachers and professors throughout my schooling. For their specific contributions to the Tomato Collection (book and all aspects of the project), a big thanks to Bill Kenner, Cynthia Simpson, Margaret Proctor, Deanna Morse, Anthony Thompson and Constance Jones.

Thank you to West Ottawa Public Schools and all the staff.

Thank you to all the teachers and schools who have allowed me to visit.

Thank you to the authors and illustrators who have given me advice, especially Mark Herrick, Jane Stroschin and Tom Woodruff.

Thank you to all my family, Kristi, Brian and Ashley Rogalske, Lori, Eric and Zachary Fox, Grandma DeMaat, Grandma and Grandpa Ditmar, and all the extended relatives.

Thank you to all my friends (sorry that's so generic).

Thank you to Mackies World, Americas First Mall for Children.

Thank you to David Sayers at the Small Business Development Center.

Thank you to Jerry Vanden Bosch at LVS Professional Services, Inc.

Thank-you to Edna Stephens at Edco Publishing, Inc.

Thank you to Tom Vranich for your support in helping make the Tomato Collection an "actual book."

Thank you to all the people currently involved in the recording of the Tomato Collection Soundtrack and the development of the Tomato Collection Interactive CD ROM.

Thank you to the many, many people who have offered suggestions, ideas, wisdom and for supporting me in so many different ways.

I apologize for not having everyone's name here that should be (if I missed you, next time you see me give me a good whack in the head).

And finally, thanks to God for making sure that his sun will always float.

the
TOMATO
collection

Kevin would love to visit your school or organization. Please feel free to contact Cooperfly Books for more information. Also contact Cooperfly Books to find out about other Tomato Collection products.

Phone -Toll Free:
1-877-9TOMATO
(1-877-986-6286)

Mailing Address:
Cooperfly Books
3148 Plainfield N.E. Suite 248
Grand Rapids, MI 49525

Internet:
www.tomatocollection.com
e-mail: kevin@tomatocollection.com

THE FUTURE OF THE WORLD IS IN YOUR HANDS.
THE HANDS OF THE FUTURE IS IN YOUR WORLD.
THE WORLD OF THE HANDS IS IN YOUR FUTURE.

The SECRET IS TO ENJOY THE DAY AND THE NIGHT
the NIGHT AND THE DAY IS THE SECRET TO ENJOY.

(THIS ISN'T 'WORKING' YET
  BUT SOMEDAY IT JUST MIGHT
    AND THEN...
      ... IT JUST MIGHT BE COOL)

good nite

THE UNEXPRESSED EMOTION

  SOMETIMES
  IN FACT, QUITE OFTEN
  A FEELING, AN EMOTION
  IT IS SO POWERFUL
  ~~THAT~~ NO WORDS CAN EXPRESS ~~ANY~~ IT ~~ON WHATEVER~~

  ONLY INSTEAD
                    THAT
  YOU ARE STUCK WITH ~~THE~~ CONTAINMENT
  HOPING, LONGING TO FIND A WAY TO RELEASE IT.

√ 9/19

THE TOM COLL